Acknowledgements:

This book is dedicated to all of the children I have taught to learn, to look into my eyes, to speak, and to hesitantly step out of their silent world of Autism and into my loud, chaotic, and unpredictable world.

I have learned far more from teaching and training up these children than they have learned from me.

"Train up a child in the way he should go; even when he is old he will not depart from it."
Proverbs 22:6.

Table of Contents

- Introduction
- ABA Strategies in the Home
- ABA Strategies in the Classroom
- ABA Strategies During a Therapy Session
- ABA Strategies in the Community
- 10 Things Your ABA Therapist Wishes You Knew
- My Personal Reinforcer List
- Appendix
- References

Introduction

If you are reading this book right now you're probably someone who is responsible for raising or teaching an individual who has Autism.

.... Or, you have absolutely no interest in Autism but thought the cover of the book was cool.

Either way, I thank you for deciding to read this book and further your knowledge about Applied Behavior Analysis.

I wrote this book to be used as a resource tool full of behavioral strategies. As a Behavior Analyst, I consult with and train all kinds of people who need ideas about how to best handle challenging behaviors. Most of the people I come into contact with have a basic knowledge of ABA and how it relates to Autism. Teachers know about ABA, Speech Therapists know about ABA, parents know about ABA, but sometimes this knowledge is full of myths, untruths, and false ideas. Some of these ideas can be odd, outdated, or potentially harmful. Without a solid understanding of what ABA is (and what it is not), then it's pretty difficult to use it effectively.

<u>So, what is ABA?</u>

Well, my technical and super educational answer would be: *Applied Behavior Analysis is a well respected, empirically sound treatment method for Autism. ABA at its core is a way to teach, manage, or reduce behaviors. ABA is not a one-dimensional concept, but rather an umbrella term that covers many strategies such as Incidental Teaching, Discrete Trial Training, and Verbal Behavior.*

Whew, what a mouthful! So what is ABA really? Well, ABA is a science composed of a variety of techniques and methods that anyone (yes, **anyone**) can use to bring about a change in behavior. ABA professionals work in the domain of behavior, not thoughts or feelings or emotions. I can't teach your child to have happy thoughts. What I can do is teach your child to exhibit happy behaviors, once you define what "happy" means to you. Make sense?

This book is intended to give the reader the confidence to implement ABA techniques and strategies. My goal is to help make ABA more accessible to everyday people. Every tip and strategy in this book is based in ABA principles and theory. All of the questions in the book are actual questions about behavior that parents, family members, teachers, or ABA therapists have asked me.

What this book is NOT is a cookbook of behavior recipes that will work with all children. Nothing about ABA is paint-by-numbers. For any behavior you want to change, ABA provides you with a multitude of interventions to try. If at first you don't succeed with one intervention, then move on to a different one. This book is filled with tips and interventions that I have used successfully to change behavior, and if you flip to the end of the book you will find a helpful guide to creating your own behavioral intervention.

I didn't spend time, money, and effort collecting all of this ABA knowledge in my brain just to throw out impressive jargon at cocktail parties (which I can totally do, by the way). Knowledge is useless unless it is shared with others. By reading this book and understanding the strategies listed in it, you will have the power to systematically and intentionally improve the behavior of your child, student, client, cousin, nephew, niece, father, sister, etc. who has Autism.

Oh, about that....ABA isn't just for individuals with Autism. Did you know that?
ABA is much bigger than a behavioral treatment method for Autism. Remember, ABA is a scientific discipline used to bring about a change in behavior. So who might need a behavioral intervention besides individuals with Autism?

Hmmm, well let's see.....

Individuals with:

Traumatic Brain Injuries
Cerebral Palsy
Cognitive Impairments
ADD
ADHD
Anxiety Disorders
OCD
Downs Syndrome
Learning Disabilities
Behavior Disorders
Speech Impairments
Developmental Delays

...And many, many more.

See, this is an all-inclusive book you are about to read. These strategies can be used with anyone.

I hope you find this book to be an informative and practical wealth of information that gives you the power to bring about positive behavior changes in the people you care about.

Good luck!

ABA Strategies in the Home

#1 Talking Back

*"My son always has to have the last word. When I tell him to do something he begins to argue or debate, and it ends with us going back and forth and him repeatedly telling me what he is **not** going to do".*

When dealing with any persistent, challenging behavior it's important to think about what is maintaining the behavior for the child: What do they get out of the behavior? If your child argues with you after hearing "No" or a statement they don't like, you are giving that child a lot of attention by arguing back with them. You are validating the child's statements by responding to them. Stop responding when your child talks back to you, and go busy yourself with something in another room. Remove your attention completely. Once the child learns that you will not argue with them, they will stop. Your word should be final. You do not need to convince your child that you mean what you say.

#2 Potty Mouth

"My son loves to say inappropriate words like "poop", "crap", or sometimes he will curse. Its very annoying and I keep telling him to stop but he won't".

It's important to make a clear distinction between what is acceptable behavior in your household, and what is not. When your child curses or says potty words you need to ignore that behavior. Act as if you cannot hear the child. When the child begins to speak appropriately, provide lots of attention and only speak to them when they are speaking to you appropriately. Do not treat potty talk as if its acceptable speech.

#3 Self-Injurious Behaviors (SIB's)

"My daughter has really bad tantrums sometimes, where she falls to the ground and will bang her head very hard against the floor. It's scary and I'm so afraid she will hurt herself. How do I handle that"?

SIB's are always a serious matter that you want to address immediately, before the behavior has the opportunity to get worse or increase in intensity. When dealing with harmful behaviors it's always recommended that you work with a Board Certified Behavior Analyst to conduct a Functional Behavior Analysis. A FBA will determine the function of a behavior. Once the function is determined, the BCBA will create a specific behavior plan that will teach the child another way to get that function met where they don't have to harm themselves. For example, if your daughter head bangs during tantrums to get your attention the behavior plan could include blocking the head banging while staying quiet and not looking directly at your daughter. Then when your daughter is calm and appropriate, you would give her lots of attention, hugs, and eye contact. **I wouldn't advise you to intervene on any harmful behavior without first conducting a FBA.**

#4 Naptime Difficulties

"My son with Autism is almost 4, but he just transitioned from a crib to a big boy bed. I'm having a lot of problems with his naps because he cries and yells until I get in the bed with him. I rub his back and calm him down, and if I try to leave the bed he starts crying again. I usually end up falling asleep in his bed with him".

Children with Autism often need consistency, structure, and routine. What you have inadvertently done is taught your child a naptime routine that ends with you cuddling him until he falls asleep. Your son's crying is his way of saying "Hey, get back here. You know our routine!" What you will need to do is create and implement a new bedtime routine and follow it consistently. Do not climb into your son's bed any longer. Read him some books, sing to him, give him a huge kiss, and then say goodnight and leave the room. Be prepared to place him back into the bed if he gets out coming looking for you.

#5 Wakes up Early

"My daughter is 3 and she has Autism. She falls asleep easily at night, but she wakes up every morning between 3 and 5 am. Everyone else in the house gets up around 7 am. When my daughter wakes up she comes and climbs into bed with my husband and I, and wants to play".

Sleep issues are common with children who have Autism. You can try changing your daughters bedtime (making it later), or doing calming activities before bed (such as massage her back) to help her sleep longer. However, it sounds like you are fine with her waking up early but not fine with her waking you and your husband up. You need to teach your daughter to stay in bed in the morning until someone comes to get her. The way you do that is by taking your daughter back to her bed every time she gets out of it in the morning. Tell her "It's not time to get up yet" the first time you put her back in bed. After that, don't keep repeating yourself, and don't give a lot of attention to your daughter. If she stays in bed until someone comes into her room to get her, you can give her a special treat such as her favorite waffles for breakfast. If she does not stay in bed when she wakes up then she is taken right back to bed each time she gets out of it, and she also doesn't get her favorite waffles.

#6 Dislikes Hugs

"My teenager with Autism has some sensory issues, and he dislikes touch. No one is allowed to touch his hair or his head, and if I try to hug him he pushes me away. Is there anything I can do about him hating hugs"?

Sensory issues can include a dislike or fear of certain textures, sounds, tastes, smells, etc. or the child may be strongly drawn to certain textures, sounds, tastes, etc. You always want to be considerate of the individual when it comes to sensory issues. You can help your son be desensitized by starting slow. Tell him you are going to touch him before you do, always touch him from the front so he can see you approaching, and pair touch with fun activities. Let your son watch his favorite movie, and briefly give him a hug while he watches the movie. Keep the hugs very brief at first, and gradually increase how long the hug is. I believe in asking children with Autism for hugs; I don't just walk up and hug them. My rule is its okay if you don't want me to hug you but you need to say "no", not just push me away or cry. If the child is nonverbal they can shake their head to indicate "no". Typically my clients tend to passively *receive* hugs rather than *give* hugs. Ultimately, it's their body and they do not have to hug me if they don't want to.

#7 Spitting

"My daughter has this new habit of spitting onto tables. I think she enjoys seeing the spit because she doesn't spit onto grass or sand, only flat, light colored surfaces. It's a disgusting habit and I want her to stop".

This is a behavior you will want to conduct a Functional Behavior Analysis on. Some children spit for sensory reasons; they enjoy the feel of spitting, looking at their spit, etc. Other children spit because of the reaction it gets from other people. The results of the FBA will determine your behavior plan. For example, if your daughter is spitting for sensory purposes then you can give her a replacement sensory activity such as spraying water onto tables with a spray bottle. I once worked with a little boy who loved to spit and I taught him to collect water in his mouth from a cup or water bottle and spit that out instead, and eventually he was only allowed to do that in the shower.

#8 Mouthing

"My child walks around the house and picks things off the ground—anything—and puts it in her mouth: Lint, pennies, cotton balls, etc. She doesn't try to chew or eat this stuff; she just wants to put everything into her mouth."

Mouthing is when children place non-food items in their mouth. I usually see this in developmentally delayed children without play skills. These children have difficulty understanding what to do with objects. You hand them a toy, and they don't know what to do with it, so it goes into their mouth. You always want to block mouthing, and don't allow the child to place random items in their mouth. In addition you will need to teach the child how to appropriately interact with objects. Teach them how to play with items, stack items, or match items. If your daughter is matching pennies, then she can't be mouthing the pennies at the same time.

#9 Screaming

"My daughter has Autism, and she is nonverbal. She screams a lot at home. If she wants to watch TV she screams until

someone turns it on. If she wants juice, she goes into the kitchen and screams until we give it to her".

Children who do not speak or communicate usually have many challenging, disruptive behaviors, like screaming. The reason why this child screams is to communicate her wants/needs. She also screams because it <u>works</u>. She knows that if she screams at you, eventually someone will give her what she wants. The first thing you want to do is stop treating her screams like words. Do not give her what she wants because she screams. You also need to teach your daughter a better way to communicate her wants and needs, such as teaching her sign language, or to point or gesture at what she wants.

#10 Masturbation

"My daughter has mild Mental Retardation, and she is 12. Recently she has started a behavior where she will rub and touch herself inappropriately. I'm concerned that my younger children will start copying this behavior. How do I handle this?"

Just like any adolescent, your daughter is curious about her body. I would advise you to teach your daughter that masturbation is a private behavior. She needs to engage in it when she is alone, and behind a closed door (such as her bedroom). You may need to place a time limit on this behavior if your daughter is masturbating excessively. Usually if adolescents are taught that masturbation is okay but not around other people, then this is an easy behavior to manage.

#11 Poor Table Manners

"My son never wants to sit down and eat his meals. He always wants to eat a few bites ad then get up from the table. When I *tell him to sit back down, he cries. He also throws his plate on the floor sometimes".*

You need to teach your son appropriate eating behaviors while at the table. Be prepared to model and practice this behavior multiple times. If your son tries to throw his plate, block this and tell him in simple language that he cannot throw things. Set a timer for a specified amount of time, such as 6 minutes, and your son cannot get up from the table until the timer goes off. If he has eaten all his food by the time the timer goes off, provide lots of praise such as "Big boy, you ate all your food!" If he hasn't eaten any food by the time the timer goes off, let him get up but don't provide any praise or reinforcement.

#12 Elopement

"My son has Autism, and he's 6 years old. Sometimes he wanders away from the house, and this really worries me. How do I get him to understand that he can't just walk off alone?"

When dealing with elopement you want to think about prevention as well as safety measures. Modify the home environment to make it safer. Install heavy duty deadbolt locks on the doors and windows. Install an alarm in the home or consider security cameras. Consider placing bells or motion detectors on all doors. Talk to neighbors and explain that you have a child who wanders, and may not respond to his/her name. Make sure close neighbors have your contact information and a photo of your child, so if your child ever wanders into their yard they can call you immediately. Start determining the triggers for your child attempting to elope. Many children display wandering behavior in the middle of the night if they can't sleep. Other children wander away from home if they see something interesting outside, such as the ice cream truck driving by. Once you have identified the triggers, teach your child replacement behaviors. If they wander in the middle of the night teach them to stay in bed when they can't sleep. If they wander outside to explore interesting items teach them that they need permission first. If the child is verbal they can request permission to go outside. If the child is nonverbal, you can make an "Outside" picture card. When the child brings you the picture card, they are allowed to go outside (with supervision). Put the picture card away at night, to signify that going outside at night is not an option.

#13 Hates Change

"My son has Autism, and he gets very upset if his day has unexpected changes. We try to keep his schedule consistent from day to day, but that isn't always possible. If we have to change his schedule he gets upset and will tantrum."

Many children with Autism can benefit from a visual schedule. You would use picture cards or photographs to create a schedule of the child's day and the schedule can be modified if the day will change. For example, if the family is going out to eat instead of eating at home, you can add a photo of a restaurant to the visual schedule. Use the schedule consistently and teach the child to follow their schedule throughout the day, so he will learn the order of his day. When schedule changes happen, it will be easier for your son if he can "see" the change visually on his schedule. Visual schedules make abstract concepts, such as the passage of time, more concrete for children with Autism.

#14 Dislikes Siblings

"My toddler has PDD and she won't play with her siblings. If I set up games and toys for the kids to play, she will walk around the room and ignore the other kids. She will only interact with the toys once her siblings leave the room. How do I get her to play with her siblings?"

If your child is ignoring or interacting inappropriately with her siblings then you need to teach your child appropriate play behaviors. You can't expect your daughter to play and interact with siblings if she has never displayed that she knows how to do so. You will need to start by placing yourself in the midst of your children and prompting them to interact with each other. Choose a simple game and help the kids take turns playing together, several times each day. Social behaviors need to be taught, and be prepared that it may take multiple practice sessions before your child starts spontaneously interacting with her siblings. Be patient as your daughter learns this new skill.

#15 Climbs Everything

"My daughter is very hyper, and she will climb anything in our house- the refrigerator, counters, the stove, the entertainment center, etc. We pull her down once we catch her climbing, but a few minutes later she's doing it again."

If your daughter is showing you that she needs to climb things, then stopping her from climbing won't be enough to get rid of this behavior. In addition to not allowing your daughter to climb you need to provide her with something to do instead, or give her a replacement behavior. Replacement behaviors are best when they resemble the original behavior. So teach your daughter that it's okay to climb onto the jungle gym at the park, climb a ladder in the garage, or climb a tree in the backyard, but it is not okay to climb furniture in the home.

#16 Imitates TV

"My son loves to imitate. He loves watching this one cartoon about a karate master, and he gets excited and runs around the house kicking at everyone. I tell him to stop, but that only works for a moment."

The good news is your son is imitating, which can be a hard skill to teach. The bad news is he is imitating things you don't want him to imitate. Explain to your son that in order to watch this specific TV show he needs to sit appropriately with quiet feet and quiet hands. If he complies and watches the show appropriately, give him a high five and tell him he's doing great. If he gets up and starts imitating karate moves, turn the TV off and tell your son that if he can't watch the cartoon appropriately then you will give him something else to do.

#17 Acting Out Behaviors

"Whenever I get on the phone my daughter demands my attention. She pulls at my shirt and whines until I pick her up. I have to rush through all my phone calls or hold her the entire time."

Your daughter's behaviors are intended to take your attention off your phone call and back onto her...and its working. Stop picking her up when she cries and whines. Create individual number cards from 1-5. When you begin a phone call, hold up the number 5. A few minutes later hold up the number 4, a few minutes later the number 3, etc. When you have gone through all the numbers, place your caller on hold and pick up your daughter briefly and give her lots of attention. Then put her down, and go back to your phone call. This lets your daughter know that whining and pulling at you will not gain your attention, but waiting appropriately is a great way to get your attention.

#18 Hates the Sound of the Doorbell

"My son has sensory issues, and he's 7. We don't have company at our home often, but when people do come to the house and ring the doorbell my son screams and goes running through the house. I have to chase him down and calm him first before I can even open the door."

You can make the doorbell a positive experience for your son. When you are inside your house and the doorbell rings, get excited. With an excited facial expression say to your son "Somebody's at the door!" Take your son with you to answer the door, and prompt him to open the door for the guest. After your son has opened the door give him a special treat, like a cookie. Over time instead of the doorbell being associated with a loud, unexpected noise and running away, your son will associate it with excitement and praise.

#19 Mistreats Family Pet

"I got my son a kitten because I read that animals are great for kids with Autism. The kitten is very friendly and sweet but my son only wants to pull the kittens tail and chase her around the house yelling. He doesn't actually play with the kitten."

You can teach your son to play nicely with his pet. Try writing a Social Story for your son that explains how to pet, care for, brush, and cuddle the kitten. Supervise your son when he is around the kitten to make sure he is interacting appropriately. Remind him to use a soft touch by modeling on his arm how he should pet the kitten.

#20 Pees in the Bed

"I toilet trained my daughter last summer, but she still pees in the bed 3-4 times a week. I cut off all fluids for her after 6 pm, but that didn't seem to help."

It isn't unusual for children with special needs to have accidents from time to time; typically developing children do this also. However, if your daughter is having accidents on a consistent basis then that's a problem. Make sure your daughter uses the bathroom before bed. After she goes to sleep, wake her up every 3-4 hours to use the bathroom. If she is already wet when you wake her up then push the time back 30 minutes. Adjust the schedule as needed to prevent her from having accidents. Once you get the schedule down and start consistently waking your daughter to use the bathroom, she will start to wake up on her own at those specific times to go to the bathroom.

#22 Won't Pick up Toys

"My 2 year old with Developmental Delay goes from room to room in the house, leaving a huge mess behind her. Every time I look up she is playing with a different toy, and just as quickly as she picks up one toy she drops it to go play with something else."

In addition to teaching your daughter to clean up, you also can lengthen her ability to attend to an object. Set up Centers in the play area of your home of a few different activities your child enjoys. Set a timer for a few minutes and direct your child to the first center. Help her to stay in that center and you can even engage in play with her. Once the timer goes off, prompt her to clean up the area and move to the next center. Over time your daughter will be able to play with toys for a longer period of time, and she will have learned that she cannot start a new activity until she cleaned up the last one.

#23 Picky Eater

"My daughter has Autism, and she has a very restricted diet. It's so hard to get her to eat. At breakfast it has to be cereal only, no milk. At lunch, it's a crust-less ham sandwich on wheat bread only. If I try and give her white bread she refuses to touch the sandwich."

Start observing the specific foods your child likes. See what they have in common: Are they cold? Mushy? Crunchy? Sweet? When introducing new foods they should be similar to what your child already eats. If your daughter loves orange juice, then a similar food would be pineapple juice. Grape juice is very dissimilar, so that wouldn't be a good choice. Broaden your daughter's diet slowly and always introduce new foods with foods she already enjoys. At first, only require her to taste the new food. Then require a bite, then 2 bites, and so on. Go slowly and provide lots of praise as your daughter tries new foods.

#24 Won't Make His Bed

"How do I get my son to make his bed in the morning?"

Make a visual schedule for your son. Write out the steps to making the bed, and you can also include pictures of each step. When your son gets up in the morning prompt him to follow the schedule to make his bed. If he follows all the steps in order to make his bed, let him pick what he wants to eat for breakfast.

#25 Won't Poop in Potty

"My daughter has Autism, and she's been toilet trained for about 2 years. She still has to wear Pull-Ups because she won't poop in the potty."

It isn't unusual that children with Autism may need separate instruction to poop in the toilet, even after they are toilet trained. A good rule of thumb is that reinforcement for pooping in the potty should be **3x** the size it is for peeing in the potty. Start keeping a written log of times of day when your daughter poops in her Pull-Up. About 10 minutes before each time, put her on the toilet and make sure she sits there. Provide praise for sitting on the toilet, but if she actually voids in the toilet have special, separate reinforcers for her that she can't get at any other time. If your child is in school, give these same recommendations to the teacher or your child will only poop in the potty at home.

ABA Strategies in the Classroom

#26 Won't Share

"One of my students has Downs Syndrome, and he gets very aggressive with the other children whenever he has to share. Almost every day he hits another child because they try to take a toy from him."

Children with special needs often need to be specifically taught appropriate social behaviors. A few times a day, do a structured play activity with this student and another peer. Select 1-3 highly preferred toys. When the child attempts to hit, block the aggression and show him what to do instead. Prompt him to say "My turn" instead of hitting. After a few moments have him give the toy to the other child while saying "Your turn". If the child begins to cry or whine, ignore that and remind him it will be his turn again soon.

#27 Talking Out in Class

"One of my students interrupts me all the time. He shouts out answers or will blurt out questions every few minutes. I remind him to be quiet but I don't know what else to do."

First, it's important to stop responding to this student when he talks out in class. Don't feed this behavior. Start paying lots of attention to this student when he is quiet. Walk over to his desk, give him eye contact, or smile at him when he is quiet. When he talks out inappropriately, do not respond. Give specific praise to other students who raise their hand ("Thank you for raising your hand, Eddie") to model for this student what he is supposed to do instead of talking out. When he does raise his hand, immediately give him attention and praise for doing so.

#28 Difficulty Transitioning

"One of my students tantrums almost everyday when its time to leave the playground. I tell the children to come line up, and he is the only one who ignores me and keeps playing. I have to go get him, and walk him inside and by then he is crying and trying to pull away from me."

Start giving this child transition statements so he knows it's almost time to go inside. Walk over to where he is, and say directly to him "In ___ minutes, we're going inside" and then walk away. Give 2-4 warnings. Once it is time to go inside, go to this child first and have him help you collect the other children. Have him walk around with you making sure all the children line up, and then let him be the "caboose" of the line.

#29 Constantly Teased

"One of my students has Aspergers Syndrome, and the other kids make fun of him a lot. How can I help him fit in better?"

One of the best ways to help a student with Aspergers fit in better with peers is to pair him with a peer to do activities together. Pair the children up during reading or math, and give them an assignment that they need to work on together to complete. Instead of letting the students freely pick partners for an activity, tell them who they will be working with. Many children with Aspergers are ignored by peers, and seen as odd or weird. By placing the children together they get a chance to interact and work together on a project, which can lead to socialization. What's most important is to not allow the other children to ignore him. Create opportunities in the day for structured interaction.

#30 Lining Up

"A student in my Kindergarten class has ADD, and when its time to line up she gets overexcited. She runs to the door, stepping on and pushing other children, and aggressively pushes the other children in line."

Instead of saying to the class in general "Go line up", have the students line up individually or gradually. Tell everyone wearing a green shirt to get in line, or everyone with black hair to go line up. Also as the children go line up tell them to hold an imaginary hula hoop around their waist. If anyone around them touches their imaginary hula hoop, they are too close and need to back up.

#31 Working Independently

"A little girl in my class has ADHD, and she always needs my help to complete her assignments. I tell the children to start working, but she just sits there staring into space until I come over and help her."

Make sure the student has written and/or visual instructions on her that explain the assignment. This student may need more than auditory directions. Circle all of the odd numbered problems on the assignment and tell the child when she gets to a circled problem she can raise her hand and you will come over and help her. However, she must try to complete the even numbered problems on her own. When you see this student independently starting her assignments, walk by her desk and give her a smile or a thumbs up.

#32 Rowdy in PE

"One of my students has Autism and he is nonverbal. He seems to really enjoy PE, but it also winds him up. By the end of PE he is usually running around the gym in circles, laughing hysterically, and sometimes gets aggressive with the other children."

Due to the physical activity in PE, the noise of the gym, and the large amount of students in the room, it can be an over-stimulating environment to a child with Autism. Allow this child short breaks during PE so he can enjoy PE and participate, but not become overstimulated. Every 10-15 minutes have the child sit down in the back of the gym, or sit outside with a teacher for quiet time. Make sure to state to the child he is just taking a break, and didn't do anything wrong. Let the child sit for a few minutes, and then take them back to join the class. Eventually you can teach the child to request a break using a break card. When you see the child getting overstimulated ask him if he needs to take a break, and then prompt him to give you the break card.

#33 Isolates During Recess

"I have a student who completely ignores the other children during recess. Instead of playing with anyone he chooses to walk around the perimeter of the playground until its time to go back inside."

Observe this child and see what activities he enjoys doing by himself. Explain to him that during recess he has to do 1 activity with a peer, and then he can do 3 of his favorite activities. So he must play kickball with a peer, and then he can collect rocks, sit on the slide, and walk around the playground alone. Once the child is doing that regularly, require that he do

2 activities with a peer, and he can do 2 of his favorite activities. Continue until the child is spending the majority of his time on the playground playing with a peer, and only a small portion engaged in solitary play. The goal isn't to completely remove his solitary play, but to reduce it.

#34 Constantly Out of Seat

"One of my students is always up out of her seat, walking around the room or talking to other students. How do I get her to stop getting out of her seat?"

Focus on the behavior you want to see, not the behavior you want to stop. For every 10 minutes that this student stays in her seat, tell her she just earned one gold star. At the end of 30 minutes if the student has earned at least 2 gold stars then allow her a special treat, such as getting to pick 1 item out of your goodie drawer (every teacher should have a goodie drawer).

#35 Initiating Conversation

"A girl in my class has PDD, and she seems to want to play with the other kids but doesn't know how. She will walk up to the other children and watch them as they play, but after a few minutes she just walks away. How can I help her interact?"

It sounds like she need help initiating social interaction with others. Create some social cue cards, and give them to this student. Keep the cards very simple, short, and sweet. Such as "Hello", "Can I play", or "Chase me". Each day hand the girl a different card and lead her over to a peer and have her read the card to start an interaction with her peers.

#36 Escaping Undesired Tasks

"A child in my class has a problem behavior of leaving his desk and walking around the room when its time to do math. If a teacher sits with him at his desk, he fights the teacher to get up out of his seat. He gets very aggressive."

Children who are trying to escape an undesired task can often exhibit very defiant, aggressive behaviors. Work in more reinforcement into math instruction time. If the worksheet has 10 problems, sit down with this student and help him do the first problem. Once he has had some success on problem #1, tell him to do problem #2 by himself and then he can take a short break. When dealing with a task the student finds very unpleasant, break up the task or reduce the difficulty level. When dealing with escape behaviors it's very important you don't allow the child's aggression to make you remove the demand completely, or you will see the aggression start to increase.

#36 Elopement

"At the end of the day, one of my students always tries to run out of the room to go get on the school bus. She knows she is supposed to wait until a teacher walks her out to the bus, but almost every day she will try and bolt out of the room and head to the bus by herself."

Don't prepare this child for the school bus (putting on her coat and book bag) until right before its time for her to go to the bus. Make sure she is engaged in an activity, and not just wandering around the classroom. If she is busy doing something it's less likely she will try and elope. Give her transition statements regularly, letting her know it's almost time to go such as "Let's read one more book and then we will walk to the bus".

#37 Lack of Eye Contact

"One of my students has Autism, and it's very hard for me to get eye contact from her. She is verbal and will make conversation with me, but she always looks down at the floor. I'm not sure how to teach her to make eye contact."

Many children with Autism avoid making or sustaining direct eye contact, even though they may be attending to you and listening to you. Start praising the eye contact this student does make, even if it's very brief. Give immediate feedback such as "Great job looking at me". Play interactive games with the student that are nonverbal, so the child must examine your face and look for cues, such as Charades, or just take turns making funny faces and have the child imitate your facial expressions. Make eye contact fun and enjoyable, and the child will begin to do it more.

#38 Inattentiveness

"How do I get my students with Autism to be more attentive in the classroom, and pay attention to what is relevant?"

Use more visuals in your teaching such as flashcards, charts, and photographs. Help your students with Autism to tune out irrelevant stimuli by minimizing it: keep the classroom free of clutter and unnecessary objects, seat distractible students up front close to the chalkboard, and modify the physical environment if you can. Use lamps instead of artificial fluorescent lighting, play calming music softly in the background, put blinds or curtains over windows, and close the door during times of day when the hallway is busy.

#39 Disrupts Others

"I teach preschool age children, and one of my students is Developmentally Delayed. During Music he refuses to sit down, wants to run around the room, and cries when he is brought back to the group. It's very disruptive to me and to the other children."

Do more to involve this child in group instruction time—give him something to do. Make him your special helper and have him pass out materials or musical instruments. Sit him close to you and give him a manipulative to hold. Let the children move around more often, such as getting up every 3 minutes to march around the room to a specific song.

#40 School Toileting Issue

"I teach 2nd grade, and one of my students won't use the toilet at school. I know she is toilet trained at home, but at school she holds it until she has an accident. This happens a few times a week."

For the best generalization success, the school toileting process needs to mirror what was taught in the home. Use the same (or similar) reinforcement schedule that was used in the home, including the same reward system. If possible, bring a few items from home and place them in the school bathroom such as a special book the child likes to read on the toilet. Making the two environments similar will help the child generalize this skill from home to school. Even with the two environments being similar, be prepared that it may take the child some time to feel comfortable using the bathroom at school.

#41 Fidgeting in Class

"I have a student with ADD and during the afternoon she gets very fidgety in her seat. She starts to swing her feet and tap her hands loudly on her desk, and it bothers the other students."

Since this is happening at a specific time of day it's a good idea to plan for it in advance. 10-20 minutes before she usually gets fidgety, send the student on an errand to another classroom. This gives her an opportunity to get up, walk around, and burn off some of that fidgety energy. When the student comes back into the classroom, have her pass out papers for you or place items in cubbies. You can also give the student sensory items to manipulate at her desk, such as a stress ball she can squeeze when she starts to feel nervous energy.

#42 No Friends

"I have a student who has a behavioral disorder. She has many behaviors that either alienate or scare off the other children. I want to help her socialize more with her peers, but it's difficult because they all avoid her."

Creating a buddy system or a small social skills group is a great way for teachers to help special needs children benefit from social interaction. A buddy system is simply pairing the child with a disability with a typical peer for parts of the school day, at lunch, or to work on a special assignment. This helps the child with a disability learn how to interact with others, and it teaches the typical children as well. A social skills group consists of putting together a few children (including the child with a disability) and having a trained facilitator guide the children through social interaction such as playing a board game.

building a puzzle, or painting a picture. If the parents provide consent, you can also explain to the class what a behavioral disorder is, and how it affects being able to play and interact with others. Educate the children about what to expect and how to react to behavioral outbursts.

#43 Refuses to Participate in Circle Time

"I'm a Kindergarten teacher, and I have two students in my class with Autism. It's very difficult to get these students to participate in Circle Time with everyone else. These students run around the room, tantrum, or are disruptive during Circle Time. What can we do to get these students to do what the other kids are doing?"

Modify the expectations for the children who have Autism. If your Circle Time is 15 minutes long, only require the children with Autism to sit and attend for 3-5 minutes. After that they can take a short break, go to a different part of the room and do an activity. Then bring them back to re-join the group. Look at the current structure of your Circle Time: Are you teaching in a variety of modalities (visual, auditory, tactile)? Do you provide opportunities for the children to stand up, move around, jump, etc? Are you providing reinforcement and praise to the children with Autism when they participate? Are you modifying tasks so the children with Autism can complete them (instead of asking them what day it is, have them point to the correct day on the calendar)? Understand that from the perspective of the students with Autism, Circle Time is just a dull part of the day where they have to sit still for an extended period of time. Do all you can to make Circle Time more fun and interesting.

#44 Raising Hand

"How do I teach a child with Autism to raise his hand in class? This is a bright child who is capable of answering questions, but even when he knows the answer he doesn't raise his hand like the other students do."

This skill will need to be taught. Start practicing hand raising in a small group setting, such as just 1-3 children. Model the behavior for the child by raising your hand, and telling the child to imitate you. When he raises his hand, provide lots of praise. When in a large group setting use a simple visual to remind the student he must raise his hand, such as a picture of an upraised arm. In addition to incorporating hand raising during instruction time, practice the skill during other parts of the day. When the students are waiting to go to lunch, ask the class "Who's ready for lunch" and prompt them to raise their hand. This will help the student with Autism generalize the skill, and learn to imitate his peers.

#45 Screaming

"How do I deal with screaming in the classroom when the student is frustrated, or upset about something?"

It's important that this student learns a better way to communicate frustration. If the child is verbal you can teach them to state their frustration ("I'm mad!") or you can show them how to request a break or a calming activity. When the child screams, redirect them to use their language or to request a break. If the child is nonverbal you can use visuals and have the child point to the visual as a way of requesting. It's important you don't provide a huge reaction to the screaming, such as becoming upset, raising your voice, or appearing visibly upset. Remain calm, and remind the student what they are supposed to do instead of screaming. If the child can be taught a more effective way to communicate, that works just as well as screaming, that is when you will see the screaming behavior diminish.

#46 Time Out

"I teach children with a variety of cognitive delays, and when the children break classroom rules we place them in Time Out. The problem is, they walk right out of Time Out; they won't stay there. This happens a lot. We have some students who we send to Time Out every day, but their behavior is still the same."

Time Out is one of the most overused and misunderstood behavioral interventions I have ever come across. I would love to rent huge billboards in cities across America that list out Time Out recommendations. I'll get to that one of these days; it's on my To Do list…..but for now, its important to understand what Time Out really means. Many people don't know when they say the phrase "Time Out" they are using an abbreviation. The full name is **Time Out from Reinforcing Activities**. You must be able to identify and then isolate the reinforcement embedded in an activity for Time Out to be effective. In other words, the "Time In" environment must be reinforcing to the child before you can implement "Time Out". The goal of Time Out is to decrease the future occurrence of a specific behavior, which makes it a punishment technique. You are trying to make a behavior go down, or **punish** a behavior. The child should learn over time that engaging in specific behaviors leads to a removal of reinforcement. If after repeatedly sending a child to Time Out the target behavior does not go down, then what you are doing is not punishing to that child. Understand that you may have to do Time Out _with_ the child. In other words if the child will not stay in Time Out, or becomes aggressive when you put them in

Time Out, you may need to stay with the child to restrain them or block them from leaving Time Out. So in a way, every time you send the child to time out you are putting yourself in Time Out as well. If that's not acceptable to you, then its time to toss the Time Out technique and come up with a new strategy.

#47 Throwing Food

"I have a child in my class with Downs Syndrome. On a regular basis, she throws her food on the floor during lunchtime. Sometimes we can stop her before she throws, but not always. She eats very fast, and once she is done eating she tosses her entire tray onto the floor."

Someone needs to be sitting with this child as she eats lunch. If she has consistently displayed this behavior then you need to place a teacher in close proximity to her at lunch time because she is very likely to throw food. When she attempts to throw food, block her from doing so and place her tray on the table. Prompt her to say or make the sign for, "All Done". Once she says the word or makes the sign, provide praise and show her how to put her tray away appropriately. You also may need to give this child something to do during lunch if she eats very fast, such as a puzzle or listening to music with headphones on.

#48 Acts Up on School Bus

"One of my students with Autism hits other children and throws things out the window on the school bus. The bus driver doesn't know what to do about this behavior, and asked for my help. I talked to the student about rules for riding the bus, but I haven't seen any difference in his behavior."

The bus driver has their hands full with driving the bus safely and probably isn't able to physically restrain students from being aggressive. There are two options for this student if they want to keep riding the bus: the child can ride the bus with an aide who restrains them from hitting or throwing things, or the child can be restrained by a safety belt while riding the bus. You could also place the student up front right by the driver, and further away from other children. Its good to explain to the child the rules of bus riding, but the explanation might be happening too far away from being on the bus for it to have any effect on behavior.

#49 Inappropriate Running

"How do I get my special needs students not to run in the hallways at school? I tell them to stop running, and sometimes they do but after a few seconds they are running again!"

The first thing you can do is avoid negative language, such as "Stop running". Use positive language, such as "Walk please". This tells the child what to do, not what to stop doing. You can also make a clear distinction between inside behavior and outside behavior. When the child runs inside, remind them that only walking feet are ok inside the school. Ask them where they can run and prompt them to answer "outside". When you are outside with the child encourage them to run and jump and play, and before you go inside give them a reminder such as "Okay remember, when we go inside of the school we use walking feet only."

#50 Doesn't Respond in A Group

"I have a student with PDD in my 3rd grade classroom, and she is very bright and does well academically. However, she only responds to a teacher if you speak to her directly or call her by name. If I give an instruction to the class, she doesn't pay any

attention. I have to call her name several times and give her the instructions again."

To help this child respond within a group, have an aide near this student when you give an instruction for the whole class. The aide should prompt the child to do what everyone else is doing. Over time, you can fade out the aide by using a simple visual such as a sign that says "Look & Listen". If you give a group instruction and the child is staring down at her desk or looking out the window and doesn't respond, walk over to her and hold up the visual. Once she sees the visual that is a reminder to her to pay attention to what the group is doing.

ABA Strategies during a Therapy Session

#51 "Vocal Stims

"One of my clients has so much vocal stimming at the table: he is constantly humming, singing songs, or making sounds. Most of the demands I give he doesn't even hear me, so he gets the question wrong. I call his name to get his attention, but he just keeps making noises."

Instead of calling the child's name, teach him what "Quiet Mouth" means. When he is appropriately quiet at the table provide specific praise ("Great quiet mouth!") and reinforcement. When he starts to engage in vocal stims tell him "Quiet Mouth" and wait for him to be quiet. Have a powerful reinforcer in his sight, and as soon as he is quiet give it to him. If this student is vocally stimming on a consistent basis, you also want to make sure he is getting enough sensory input during the session. Take 2-3 sensory breaks and let him move around, jump, climb, etc, so his body is calm and he is better able to attend to you.

#52 Hysterical Giggling

"I have a client I see as soon as he gets out of school. He has this new behavior where he laughs at the table. He slumps down in his chair, plays with any materials I put on the table, and giggles non-stop. How do I get his attention?"

Since you see this client after school, he is probably overstimulated from his day. It sounds like he is having difficulty transitioning from school to therapy. Before you start the session, give the child a sensory break where he does calming, organizing activities. Examples include kneading dough, punching Play Dough, water play using his feet, or relaxation deep-breathing. When dealing with sensory caused behaviors you want to give the child what he needs before he starts to act up, otherwise you could accidentally reinforce his inappropriate behavior.

#53 Won't Stay in Seat

"How do I get the kids I work with to sit down in their chair during a session?"

If the child has never learned to sit and attend then you need to teach the skill. Write an ABA program for attending and reinforce appropriate sitting. If the child is capable of sitting and just refusing to do it, then you need to look at your teaching. Is the child getting enough reinforcement? Are you asking them to do things that are too hard? Are you giving them frequent breaks? If your teaching is on point, the child shouldn't be motivated to continue jumping up out of their seat.

#54 Grabby Hands

"I have one client who is very touchy-feely with my materials. Especially if I'm using new cards or materials, as soon as I place them on the table she grabs for them and wants to play with them. If I take them from her she gets upset."

There are different ways of learning, and some kids are tactile learners. They like to touch and manipulate things to learn about them. Allow your client to touch and look at your cards and materials, just not during instruction time. You can tell her that either before or after the session she can play with your cards, but not while she is working. You could even use her interest in the materials as a reinforcer and have her work to get several seconds to look through and touch your cards.

#55 Throwing Materials

"I work with a little girl at school, and when she gets frustrated she throws the cards off the table. I don't know if I should have her go and pick them up, because that's wasting time. I only get an hour to work with her."

I agree that if you only have a limited amount of time you don't want to tell the child to pick up multiple cards over and over again. Try changing the format of your session. Sit on the floor with the child and instead of placing cards in front of her on the floor, hold the cards up in the air so she doesn't need to touch them. Or you can do all expressive tasks, so no materials are needed. If you know she is likely to throw things if you put out materials then don't give her the opportunity to do so.

#56 Loses Skills Quickly

"One of my clients is super smart and masters targets very fast. But when we go back and do post- checks on old targets, she can't do any of them anymore. What do we need to change so she remembers what she learned?"

It's common that kids who learn skills very fast during ABA therapy, can also lose skills very fast. You need to add more maintenance into her program. Have one session per week where you work on nothing but mastered targets. You can also increase the ratio between current targets and mastered targets in a typical session. For every 4 new targets you ask her, ask 3 mastered targets. This way she is constantly working on old targets, instead of learning something and then doing nothing with that skill for weeks.

#57 Slow Progress

"I work with a little boy who is 3, and learns things very slowly. He has about 8 targets that we have been trying to teach him for months. It seems like he should be further along by now. Some days he does great, and then the next day he will get all zeros."

I like to call this a *troubleshooting* issue. Most of the new clients who contact me need help with troubleshooting. Troubleshooting is needed when something is going wrong, but nobody knows what, or why. You definitely want to reach out to a Board Certified Behavior Analyst for help with troubleshooting because so many things could be causing this child to make slow progress. The tasks could be too hard, there could be inconsistency in how the therapists are teaching, the mastery criteria could be too strict, attention and focus could be an issue, etc. It sounds like a behavioral issue, because you say that sometimes the child does great and sometimes he doesn't….that sounds like "I don't want to do this" and not like "I don't know how to do this".

#58 Saliva Play

"I have a new client who has Autism, and also cognitive impairments. He has a behavior where he collects spit in his mouth, and then he stretches it, rubs it on his arms, or rubs it on his face. All of his therapists wear gloves, but how do we get him to stop doing this?"

This is a sensory issue, and you should create a replacement behavior so this child can get sensory input in a more appropriate way. It's important that the replacement behavior be comparable to playing in his saliva. His saliva is easily produced at a moments notice, and always ready. So allowing the child to play in water wouldn't be a good choice because you have to get the water ready and take the child to the water. By that time, he could have lost interest and started playing with his saliva. A good choice would be an oral chewie, such as a chewable tube that can be worn around the neck. It's easy access and intended to go in the mouth, so it's very comparable to saliva. Oral chewies can be purchased in all kinds of colors, textures, and you can even freeze some of them. Whenever this child starts to play with his saliva, immediately redirect him to his chewie.

#59 Biting

"I'm an ABA Therapist for a 2 year old who is nonverbal. He is a biter, and he has bitten all of the therapists. How should we handle this?"

Aggressive behaviors should be addressed immediately. You will need to have a Board Certified Behavior Analyst conduct a Functional Behavior Analysis to determine the cause of this behavior. When dealing with a biter you want to always have at the front of your mind that this child could bite you at any moment. Don't place any part of your body near the child's mouth, avoid wearing long sleeved shirts, do not turn your back on the child, and minimize close physical contact until the biting is under control. <u>Be careful.</u> Since this child is nonverbal, this biting is likely a form of communication. Once you get the results of the FBA, it will also be important to implement a communication system for this child such as sign language.

#60 Parents In Session

"How do I ask the parents not to come into the room during my session? It really distracts the child, and when his parents leave the room he cries for a really long time."

Many parents want to observe their child's ABA therapy to learn what the therapist is doing, make sure their child is ok, or just evaluate progress. Explain your concerns to the family and suggest they video tape your sessions instead. Video taping has a few advantages over observation. The obvious advantage is having Mom or Dad in the room is usually very distracting, whereas videotaping can be done quite discreetly. Another advantage is that if a parent is observing you during a session they need to be quiet and silently watch to be as minimally distracting as possible. But if the session is taped, you and the parents can view the tape together and they can ask you as many questions about the session as they would like.

#61 Tantrums With Therapist

"I have been working with a 4 year old girl about 2 months, and when I show up to her house for a session she starts crying and whining. I ignore those behaviors and we start our session but then her crying becomes a full tantrum. It takes at least 20 minutes to calm her down, and this happens a lot."

It's normal that these kiddos won't always be excited to see the therapist arrive. Let's face it, you represent work. It's not so normal that this behavior is happening on a consistent basis, and the crying escalates into a tantrum. Before beginning therapy with any new client, you always want to develop a solid bond, or rapport. This is done by pairing yourself with fun things that the child enjoys like DVD's, swinging on a swing, ice cream, etc. For this client you need to go back and do more pairing for a few days, and then slowly ease work back in.

#62 Pushes Away From Table

"One of the kids I work with gets frustrated a lot during sessions, and when he does he pushes away from the table, and scoots his chair back across the carpet."

Try sitting on the floor during your sessions. Place the child in a corner, and sit in front of him so that he cannot get past you. When the child gets frustrated, block any aggression attempts and redirect the child back to the task.

#63 Tunes Therapist Out

"What should I do when my clients tune me out during a session (ignore me, stare into space)?"

Increase your speed of instruction; start to speak more quickly and in an animated tone of voice. In addition switch up the reinforcers you are using. State a demand, and if the child doesn't respond within a few seconds remove the reinforcer from their sight and move on to the next demand. This will show the child that they have a short amount of time to respond to you or they miss out on some really cool reinforcers.

#64 Scrolling

"My client sometimes has this behavior where he will give me several answers to a question, but only one is right. If the right answer is "dog", he will say "cat/bird/dog". How do I fix this?"

This behavior is called scrolling. It's difficult to correct, but you definitely want to nip it in the bud so the child doesn't think he is giving you the right answer. As soon as the child starts to give you the wrong answer correct them immediately, talking over them if you need to. Children can also scroll receptively, such as when using sign language. In those situations you would just block the child from making the wrong sign, and immediately prompt the correct sign. Do not allow the child to continue giving you the wrong answer.

#65 Resists HOH Prompting

"When I try and use Hand Over Hand prompting with my client, she gets upset and pulls her hand away. How do I show her the right answer without causing her to escalate to a tantrum?"

HOH prompting is a very invasive prompt. For some children (such as sensory avoiders) it can actually be uncomfortable or possibly painful. If the child is recoiling from your physical touch, you can still prompt. You can use modeling, gestural, proximity, or size prompts. With modeling, you would show the child what you want them to do. With gestural prompting, you point or gesture to the correct answer. With proximity prompting, you place the correct answer very close to the child, and place the incorrect answers further away. With size prompting you exaggerate the size of the correct answer compared to incorrect answers, such as using a large flashcard for the correct card, and index cards for the incorrect cards.

#66 Hates Being Wrong

"I work with a child who gets frustrated and cries when she misses answers, or when she starts doing badly during a session. She only wants to do things that are easy for her to do."

These kiddos are children first, before any diagnosis. So you will sometimes see their unique personalities come out in interesting ways. This child sounds like a perfectionist, and that personality type enjoys contacting success. What you need to do is modify how you teach so this child contacts success more often. A great way to do this is to use errorless learning. You would provide a 0 second prompt delay between the demand and the prompt. So if you are holding up a flashcard of a cat that you want the child to label, you would say "What is it? Cat." You would immediately prompt the child so they don't have an opportunity to give you an incorrect answer. When using errorless learning it's always important to gradually fade out the prompt delay from 0, to 2, to 3-5 seconds so the child doesn't become prompt-dependent.

#67 Destroys Materials

"How do I get my clients to stop tearing, ripping, or chewing on my materials (flashcards, photos, etc.)?"

I usually laminate my materials that I use often, it's just an easy safeguard just in case you have a bad session where the child gets very upset and wants to destroy your property. You can also teach the child to have quiet hands at the table. When you give the demand "Quiet Hands" the child should place their hands flat on the table or fold them. If the child's hands are folded they can't rip up your flashcards.

#68 Won't Work for Anything

"It's really hard to find reinforcers for my client. He will work for something for a day or two, and then he doesn't want it anymore. I'm constantly having to buy new toys."

Choosing, selecting, and testing reinforcers takes skill and patience but the payoff is huge. Your client's interests and likes will change over time; that is the reality. It is normal that these kiddos will work for high fives on Tuesday, and by Friday they don't care about earning high fives anymore. You should always have a supply of reinforcing items with you that are interesting and vary in size, texture, color, etc. Don't just show up to a session and grab what is in the home and try and use that as a reinforcer. Be prepared to change the reinforcers frequently depending on the child's interests. You don't always have to buy your reinforcers. Activities, games, video clips, songs, sounds, social praise, affection, and attention can all be powerful reinforcers, and most of those cost nothing!

#69 Won't Vocally Imitate

"How do I get my client to imitate words? He is nonverbal, and we are trying to teach him to imitate language. He can imitate actions, just not words."

This is a common problem. It isn't unusual for a vocal imitation program to take weeks or even months before the child starts responding. When first teaching this skill reinforce ANY sound the child makes. I mean anything...a yawn, clucking their tongue, babbling, etc. Treat it like language. Over time, the child will make the connection between making sounds and getting their reinforcer. Then all you need to do is shape their response, by only reinforcing sounds, and eventually only words. Don't get discouraged or frustrated if progress is slow. Stay focused, use powerful reinforcers, and keep at it.

#70 Perseveration

"I'm the ABA Therapist for a 7 year old girl with Autism. She gets very anxious sometimes during a session, and will start to

bug me for her reinforcers. She will ask me for the same item over and over until I give it to her. I try telling her that she needs to wait, but that doesn't stop her from repeatedly asking me for her reinforcer."

This behavior is called perseveration. It can sometimes be caused by anxiety, or other times it could have a behavioral cause (the child asks the same question repeatedly to gain attention from you). When the child asks for something, address it _once_. If you are in the middle of a session and the child asks for a reinforcer you can say "It's not time for that". Once you have addressed the question do not answer it any more. Continue with the session and ignore the perseverative behavior. Be prepared that the child may ask you for the reinforcer much more than they usually do once you start ignoring the behavior: that is called an extinction burst.

#71 Puts Feet On Table

"What can I do to get my client to stop putting his feet up on the therapy table during our sessions?"

When the child attempts to put their feet up on the table, tell them "Quiet Feet" and prompt them to place their feet flat on the floor. Start looking for opportunities to praise the child for independently having quiet feet. Anytime you are at the therapy table and the child is sitting appropriately, tell them they are doing a great job of having quiet feet.

#72 Won't Come to Table

"I have a new client who doesn't always listen to me. I let her take lots of breaks during the session, and when I tell her to come back to the work table she ignores me. I almost always

have to go get her and bring her back to the table and physically prompt her to sit down."

Before you send the child on a break, set a timer and tell the child when the timer goes off the break is over. Give the child a few transition warnings such as, "It's almost time to come back to the table." Before the timer goes off, set a reinforcer on the table. If the timer goes off and the child comes back independently, provide praise and let them access the reinforcer. If the timer goes off and the child ignores it, remove the reinforcer and prompt the child to come sit down.

#73 Doesn't Respond to Name

"My client doesn't respond when I call her name. I can be standing right in front of her and she won't look at me, or come to me."

Teaching a child to respond to their name typically means they look at you when they hear their name. If you want the child to come to you when her name is called, you have to specifically teach that. To get her to look at you, write an eye contact program where when the child hears her name she knows to give you eye contact. At first, only require very brief eye contact. Eventually you want her to be able to sustain the gaze for a few seconds. A very common mistake many therapists make is they use the child's name so much that the child just tunes it out. You shouldn't be saying the child's name constantly in a session. If you want the child to stack blocks, don't say "Carrie, stack blocks." It will be much easier to teach this child to respond to her name if you use it sparingly.

#74 Getting Parents On Board

"Most of the families I work with are pretty involved in their child's therapy, but there's this one family who's very uninvolved. Its hard to get them to follow through with behavioral strategies, and sometimes they actively undo what it took me weeks to teach."

Not every family you work with will be on board with treatment. ABA Therapy needs active involvement from the people closest to the child in order to be the most successful. You want to include the parents as part of the treatment team, even if you have to convince them why this is important (and you might have to do that). The parents should know what programs you are teaching, what reinforcers are effective, what strengths the child has, etc. A great way of getting uninvolved parents on board is to give them a goal to teach their child. It could be a very simple goal, such as teaching the child to use a napkin when eating. Give the parents the goal, use modeling and feedback to help them learn how to use ABA to teach the skill, and be sure to provide reinforcement for their effort. Parents who feel they are a part of the treatment team tend to be more involved.

#75 Aggressive Towards Siblings

"My client has a baby brother who tries to interact and play with him all the time. Most of the time my client will just walk away from his brother, or push him away if he gets too close. How can I get the kids to play together appropriately?"

When it comes to Autism, it's very common that appropriate social skills must be taught. Your client isn't likely to stop being aggressive towards his brother until he learns what to do instead. During your sessions, take about 10-15 minutes to do an activity with the 2 boys. Have them color together, play a game, or put a puzzle together. Model and reinforce appropriate social behaviors like good eye contact, sharing, and nice, gentle touch. If your client tries to aggress towards his brother, block the aggression and show him what to do instead. Over time and with much practice, your client will learn how to interact with his baby brother in an appropriate way.

#76 Hand Washing Issues

"One of the kids I work with loves washing his hands. He's very compliant about washing hands, but he never knows when he's done. He will just keep standing at the sink with his hands under the water until I turn the water off."

Don't turn the water off for your client. It sounds like he has become prompt dependent, and he doesn't think he is done until you shut off the faucet. Give your client an auditory prompt, such as "1,2,3...Off!" Once you say "off" use gestural prompting (try to avoid touching him since he's already prompt dependent) to get the child to turn off the faucet. Remember to fade out this prompt over time, by moving further and further away from the child as he washes his hands. You can also say the auditory prompt in a softer and softer tone, to fade it out over time.

#77 Whispering at The Table

"How do I handle whispering at the therapy table, when I ask the child a question? If the answer is right do I still reinforce her?"

Only reinforce behavior you want to see increase. If you want the child to stop whispering, then no you definitely don't want to reinforce it. If the child whispers a response to you, tell them to speak louder. I usually tell a child something like "Talk like me", as I speak in a loud voice. If the child raises their voice, provide praise and reinforcement. Sometimes the child won't imitate my voice tone, and they keep whispering. If that happens, then I don't provide any reinforcement and we move on to a receptive task.

ABA Strategies in the Community

#78 Elopement

"My niece has Autism, and sometimes she wanders away from me in public. It's scary because she doesn't respond to her name, so I can yell her name out but she won't come back. Even if I look away for a few seconds, that's all the time she needs to wander away."

Elopement is a serious issue in the Autism community. There are many things you can do to prevent your niece from wandering. Before you go out in public with your niece, explain to her where you are going. Use simple language at her cognitive level and talk about your expectations for her behavior. Explain that she needs to stay near you, may need to hold your hand, and cannot walk away from you without asking first. Some children wander away when they see an interesting object. Some children wander away because it's loud and crowded, and they are seeking a quiet place. Pay attention to how she acts before she attempts to elope, such as covering ears, walking very slowly behind you, staring intently at items or objects, etc. Be on the alert so you can step in when you see a trigger. Bend down to her level and ask if she needs to take a break. If she is verbal she can learn to request a break. If she is nonverbal you can teach her to hand you a break card, and when she does she can have a supervised break. Particularly in public settings like festivals, malls, or outdoor concerts, children with Autism may elope to escape from noise and large crowds. Teach her to request a supervised break instead of just wandering off.

#79 Haircuts

*"My son absolutely **hates** going to get his haircut, and the entire process is horrible for both of us. He cries, he screams, and he makes it very hard for the barber to give him a good haircut because he won't stay seated in the chair."*

Create a Social Story of the haircut process, and start teaching it to your son well in advance of his next haircut. Use actual photos of the barber shop, the chair, the clippers, etc. Write a short sentence explaining each photo, and put all the photos together to create a book. It can be very helpful for children with Autism to know what to expect from unpleasant situations. Even after you use the picture story to explain what happens during a haircut, you may need to pair reinforcement to the haircut experience so it isn't so unpleasant for him. You can do this by packing a bag of his favorite items and goodies, and take them with you to the barber. As your son accomplishes each step of the haircut process (sits in the chair, allows a cape to be placed on him, etc.) you can provide him with a reinforcer.

#80 Won't Use Public Restrooms

"My daughter is 5 and she is toilet trained, but she often has accidents when we are out in public because she doesn't like using public toilets."

Create 2 photo strips of the toileting steps and hang one up in the bathroom at home, and take one with you when you go out in public. Your daughter might dislike public bathrooms because they are different. Bringing the photo strip from home into public bathrooms is like bringing a piece of "known" into an "unknown" environment, and should help your daughter feel more comfortable.

#81 Covers Ears

"I babysit a girl with Autism, and when we go out in public she will cover her ears and make noises if we are in a loud or crowded place. How do I get her to stop doing that?"

Due to the noise and many people in her proximity, it sounds like she is becoming over-stimulated and unconformable. By covering her ears and making sounds she is trying to tune out what is going on around her. You can try and avoid very crowded places, or if you can't do that you can hang out in a private, secluded area while out in public. If you are at the mall instead of sitting in the food court, find a quiet corner and sit down together facing away from people. You can also let her wear headphones or MP3 ear buds while out in public so she can listen to calming music.

#82 Grocery Store Tantrums

"I try to avoid taking my son into the grocery store, but sometimes we have to run in to grab something. He always wants me to buy him candy, and I tell him no but then he begins to tantrum. He seems to think that every time we walk into a grocery store that he will get a candy bar."

You are right, that's exactly what your son thinks....and he's correct. Over time you have taught him that: tantrum+ grocery store=candy bar. Here's how to correct that: When your son begins to request candy, tell him firmly that he cannot have a candy bar. If he begins to cry, falls to the floor, throws things, etc, ignore these behaviors and continue on with your shopping. Block as many of the behaviors as you can (block his arm if they go to knock something over), without giving him eye contact or reprimanding him. If he quiets down, even for a second, you can give attention then. This shows him that misbehavior gets no attention, and still doesn't get him out of the store. If you are okay with him having candy but just want him to ask nicely, then explain that to him. Tell him if he behaves inside the store that you will buy him a candy bar on the way out. It's important to understand the difference between **bribery** and **reinforcement.** Bribery does not work. Bribery is offering something to the child to stop a behavior *once the behavior has already begun.* Such as, "If you stop screaming you can have candy". The reason this doesn't work is because you are actually teaching the child that in the future if they want candy, tantrumming is how to get it. If you want to make sure you are using reinforcement and not bribery, then be sure to let the child know in advance (such as when getting out of the car) what expectations you have for them, and what happens if they behave appropriately. If the child is appropriate, they get the reinforcer. If not, they don't. Don't bargain with the child, or plead with them to behave.

#83 Stimming in Public

"What's a good way to handle stimming in public? My grandson flaps his hands when we go to the mall."

If I am in a social setting with a client and they start to engage in self-stimulatory behaviors, I will tell them to have quiet hands. I will then redirect them to an appropriate replacement behavior, such as pushing or carrying something. If their hands are full, they can't flap them. You do want to be careful not to set unrealistic demands on your grandson, so don't expect him to be inside a mall for hours with quiet hands. Allow him short breaks every 20 minutes or so to find a private spot and flap his hands. Stims serve an important function for children with Autism, so it's unreasonable to expect him to stop stimming completely. It's much more reasonable to expect him to *limit* his stimming in public.

#84 Talking Loudly

"When I take my client out to eat, he likes to squeal and talk very loudly and he also laughs very loudly. What can I do to teach him not to shout or be loud in public?"

Teach your client to use an indoor voice inside, and an outdoor voice outside. Before entering the restaurant, remind him that he will have to talk quietly once he's inside. A fun activity I do with some of my kiddos is before we go into a building or store we take a deep breath and yell to use up all of our outside voice. If there are people around you can do this inside the car, but if no one is around go ahead and shout. Its fun! Then we walk into the store and practice using our soft, indoor voice. We also yell once we leave the store. This makes talking quietly seem like a fun game instead of a rule.

#85 Trouble Leaving Stores

"If I take my daughter into a store she really likes, she tantrums when its time to leave. It's really embarrassing, and I'm not sure how to avoid this reaction from her. She is 4 and has PDD."

Be sure to give plenty of transition statements to your daughter before you leave the store such as, "We are leaving in 2 minutes." Once it is time to leave the store, race your daughter to the car. Use an animated facial expression, and a very excited tone of voice as you say, "Ready, Set...Go!" This simple game will distract your daughter from having a tantrum, and it also gives you a chance to provide reinforcement to her. If she beats you to the car (which she will...let her win!) then give her a huge hug for winning the race. Now when its time to leave a store your daughter will get excited to race you, not upset about leaving.

#86 Mouthing Items off Ground

"When I take my youngest child to the park he walks around picking things up off the ground and putting them straight into his mouth."

This behavior is called mouthing. You will want to closely observe your son at the park, and when he bends down to pick something up block him from doing so and tell him what to do instead. If he bends to pick up trash, lint, or debris, block him and say something like, "Oh that's trash, yucky!" and redirect him to go play. If he bends down to pick up food items, ask him if he is hungry. If so provide him with easy access to a snack, by putting a baggie filled with goodies in his pocket. If he has easy access to a snack, then that will compete with his desire to eat food off the ground.

#87 Trying New Places

"Should I avoid taking my child with Autism into new public places we don't normally visit, like a museum or amusement park, if he shouts, makes noises, and wants to leave quickly? Is it better to just leave him at home?"

You don't have to always take your son to places he knows and is comfortable with, but you will have to modify your expectations when you take him somewhere new. If you take him to a place he has never been before, explain to him where you are going before you get there. Once you arrive, take him in, walk around, and then walk back out. Give him a few minutes to adjust to the place, the people, the sights, and the sounds. When you see he is calm, walk back in. Follow his lead, he may want to go in but sit on a bench in a quiet area. That's fine. Or he may want to stay outside and observe people. Allow him to get comfortable with the new place in his own time, and don't try and rush him to go inside. It may take a few visits like this before your child can easily walk into the location with no behaviors.

#88 Sharing At the Playground

"When I take my daughter to the playground she loves to swing, but when it comes time for her to get off the swing and give another child a turn she whines or cries."

Help your daughter learn to share the swing by practicing turn taking. Let her swing for a few minutes, and then tell her to get down. If she won't get down, physically prompt her to get off the swing. Have her push another child on the swing to redirect her out of crying or whining. Praise her for playing nicely. After a few minutes let her get back on the swing, and see if you can find another child to push her on the swing. If not, you can push her. Turn taking is a prerequisite to sharing, so the more you practice "My Turn/Your Turn" with your daughter the better she will be at sharing with her peers.

#89 Waiting

"How do I get my daughter to be patient when the whole family is out shopping? When she's ready to leave a store, she is ready to go! How do I get her to understand that we can't leave the store until we get everything we need?"

Firstly, you may need to modify your expectations of her behavior. How long are you expecting her to patiently wait? If the family is shopping for hours and hours, that's an unrealistic amount of time. Try to minimize the amount of time your daughter has to wait for the family to finish shopping. Before you leave the house to go shopping, take a timer with you. Start the timer once in the store, and tell your daughter how long you will be in the store (e.g. "We will leave in 15 minutes."). You can show the timer to your daughter every few minutes to remind her that it's almost time to leave. Once the timer goes off leave the store. Praise your daughter for doing a great job waiting and being so patient.

#90 Dining Out

"It's hard to go out to eat as a family because my oldest son has Autism, and he's very disruptive inside restaurants. He throws food; he pours his soda on the floor....he just makes a mess. It's easier to just stay at home."

It may be easier to stay at home, but the thing about challenging behavior is they won't get any better until you intervene on them. If your son has poor table manners at home, then he will have poor table manners in public. Any behavior problem you see in the home will be magnified in public. So a good strategy is to start working on this skill at home. During mealtimes at home start practicing good table manners. Teach your son how to use a napkin, keep his eating area clean, and to be polite. It may be helpful to write these rules down so there is a list your son can refer to. When you go out to a restaurant take the rules with you, and remind your son before you walk inside of you expectations for his behavior. Use modeling at the table to show him what to do, and block any attempts to throw food. It's hard for many children with Autism to wait for food at a restaurant, or to continue to sit at the table once they are done eating. Plan for this in advance by bringing a simple activity your child can do at the table (like a puzzle), or take your son outside and let him walk around for a little bit and stretch his legs. Just being able to periodically get up and move makes it a lot easier for children with Autism to dine out at restaurants.

#91 Won't Hold My Hand

"I do Community Outings with one of my clients every week, and we visit different places around town. He never wants to hold my hand in public, and if I try and grab his hand he pulls away. I have to hold his hand though, because he wanders."

I have worked with some kids with Autism who couldn't stand holding hands. These were kiddos who didn't like lots of physical contact. It definitely can be a safety issue if your client wanders, so one thing you can try is holding the child's wrist instead of his hand. I have done this with some clients. I will hold onto their wrist as we walk together in public because they don't want to hold my hand. Or, you can teach the child to stay close to you in public. Start practicing this skill in the home first. Walk around the backyard or living room while holding some reinforcers. Verbally remind the child to stay near you. If you place out your arm and can easily touch the child, give them a reinforcer. If not, direct them to come near you and don't provide reinforcement. Eventually the child will have learned to stay within arms reach of you. Once they have learned the skill, start practicing it outside of the house.

#92 Rowdy in The Car

"My son hits his siblings when we are riding in the car. I used to turn around and go back home if he started hitting, but I can't always do that. How can I stop him from hitting while I'm driving a car?"

Change what happens when your son doesn't hit his siblings, and is appropriate. If he rides in the car appropriately and keeps his hands to himself, turn to his favorite radio station or play his favorite CD. That way you are providing incentive for him to behave appropriately, instead of just reacting when he behaves inappropriately. In addition, you can give each child a book to read or an object to play with while they ride in the car so they have something to do instead of hit each other.

#93 Criticisms from Others

"When I take my son out in public (who has Autism) sometimes people stare or even make negative comments about his behaviors. He might not even be doing anything; sometimes he's just stimming. I feel like I should say something so they know he's not just being bad."

Parents choose to handle this common problem in different ways. I know of many parents who decided to make little cards that say something like "I'm not misbehaving, I have Autism", to give to people in public who are rude or judgmental. I have been in public with clients who were having a tantrum or meltdown, and if people ask me what's wrong with the child or make disparaging comments (which has happened) I just smile and keep it short and sweet: "He's fine, thanks." You don't owe an explanation of your child's behavior to anyone, despite how bad other people may make you feel.

#94 Vacations

"What can I do to make travel easier for my child with Autism? We haven't been anywhere as a family in a long time, and I'm worried about how my son will react to his routine being completely different."

There are many things you can do to make vacations easier for your son. Notice I said easier...please don't expect a completely pain-free, perfect trip. Even parents of typical children deal with all kinds of stress during vacations and trips. The first thing that would be helpful is talking to your son about the vacation way before it begins. Create a Social Story about where you are going, what a vacation is, and how things will be very different but also very fun. If you are going to a popular vacation spot, such as Disneyland, show your child pictures of the destination and point out all the rides and fun things to do. Create a visual daily schedule for your son to use while on vacation. Especially if he has a daily schedule at home, this sense of familiarity will help him be comfortable while far away from home. Lastly, pack a few items from home to take with you while on vacation. Such as a favorite stuffed animal, or your son's favorite blue plate he always eats his snack on. Little touches of home can make your son feel at ease during vacations, and lessen anxiety.

#95 Shopping in The Mall

"My son is 8, and he loves going to the mall with me. The reason he likes going so much is because there are about 4 toy stores he likes to go into. If I try and walk past these stores without going in, he cries and whines to enter the store. How can I get him to understand that we aren't going to the mall just for him and we can't always go into these stores?"

Before you leave your house to go to the mall, you need to decide if you want to visit none, some, or all of his favorite stores. Write a list of the places you will visit inside the mall. If your son can read, the list could say: "Clothing store/Toy store/Food Court/Shoe store". If your son can't read, you can make a visual schedule. You can use photos of the stores. Using a list or schedule of where you will go in the mall and in what order will help you in many ways. It will let your son know how long he will be at the mall, and it will let your son know how many of his favorite stores he gets to visit (if any), and when. If he starts repeatedly requesting to go to the toy store, show him on the schedule when that will happen. Also, it's important that you don't take your son into the toy stores after he whines or cries. His whining and crying is his way of communicating his want to you, "*I want to go in that store*". In return, you can communicate your want to him, "*I want to keep shopping, we don't have time to stop in that store*", by ignoring his crying and whining and continuing to walk past the store.

#96 Pulling Hair

"I have a client who I take to the park once a week. He has this behavior where he walks up to little girls and pulls their hair. The other child usually cries or screams and runs away from him. This also causes adults at the park to make rude comments about my client. How should I handle this?"

Aggressive behaviors should always be treated quickly. I suggest you contact a Board Certified Behavior Analyst to conduct a Functional Behavior Analysis to determine the cause of this behavior. It's likely that this behavior is happening because your client doesn't know what to do instead of pulling hair, and because he gets a big reaction when he pulls hair. If the little girls are crying, yelling, screaming, or running away from your client, those might all sound like negative reactions to us, and not very reinforcing. But to your client if he is seeking an attention response then he just got a big one. Teach your client how to initiate social interaction with peers, such as walking up to these girls and saying "Hello". Follow your client as he approaches other children, and if he tries to pull their hair block his hands. Prompt him to give a greeting instead. It sounds like your client is doing this for an attention response, but you can't be absolutely certain of that without completing a FBA.

#97 Going to Church

"We stopped taking our daughter to church several months ago because her behaviors were so disruptive during service. She would cry, make high pitched sounds, and refuse to stay seated. Am I expecting too much of her to be able to attend church with the family, or should I keep leaving her at home?"

No, you aren't expecting too much. You may want to modify your expectations though. Instead of expecting your child with Autism to be able to quietly sit and attend for the duration of an entire church service (something that even typically developing children struggle with), create adjustments for her. Bring small fidget items that your daughter can manipulate as she sits, or allow her to wear headphones and listen to music. Give her breaks periodically where you take her outside and let her walk around, or run and jump. Be sure to provide reinforcement to your daughter when she is sitting quietly and appropriately, even if it's only for a few minutes. Whisper in her ear how proud you are of her, and how nicely she is sitting. If she starts to engage in vocal stims, remind her she must have a quiet mouth in church. When you take her outside for breaks, tell her that is the time to have a "happy mouth"—meaning she is free to shriek, squeal, and make sounds. I know many families feel embarrassed taking children with Autism to church because they don't want to interrupt other peoples worship experience. I have taken clients to church before, and what I have found is that if you are open with people and tell them in advance that the child may act differently, stand up, or make sounds, people tend to be understanding about it. I usually say something like "We're working on being quiet during church, so he may make some odd sounds or noises today. I appreciate your patience."

#98 Visiting the Doctor

"When we go to the doctor's office we always have to wait at least 30 minutes. My son is okay for the first few minutes, but then he starts to bother other people, throw things, or stim. The waiting room is pretty bland and boring so I can see why he's bored, but I can't do anything about how long we have to wait."

You can plan for these doctors' visits in advance. Make a sensory box or bin that you take with you to the doctor's office. A sensory bin is just a small, portable container that you fill with sensory items your son finds pleasurable, such as beads, seashells, pebbles, beans, pasta, etc. Don't wait until your son gets bored and starts to act up. As soon as you sit down in the waiting room, bring out a sensory box for him to play with. Get involved in his play to help keep him entertained. Pour the beans over his hand, listen to the seashells, count the pebbles, or name the colors of the pasta. Provide praise to your son as he continues to wait appropriately for the doctor, and tell him he's doing a great job.

#99 Ignores Demands

"When I take my daughter with me to visit friends, or when we go visit family, she likes to ignore me if I tell her to do something. I have to tell her over and over to do something before she will listen. Sometimes my family members say I'm being too hard on her and should just let her be, but I want her to know that just because we're not at home doesn't mean she doesn't have to listen to me."

You are right; no matter what environment you are in it's not okay for your daughter to ignore you. Use 3 Step Prompting with your daughter to gain compliance when she isn't responding to your demands. Three step prompting can best be understood by remembering the following sequence: **Tell, Show, Do. Tell-** Give a demand to her, such as "Clean up the toys". Wait 3-5 seconds for her to begin to comply. If she complies at this point, provide praise and/or reinforcement. If not, move to step 2. **Show-** Repeat the demand, while modeling or gesturing what you want her to do. Say "Clean up the toys like this" as you actually pick up a few toys and put them away. Wait 3-5 seconds for her to begin to comply. If she complies at this point, provide praise and/or reinforcement, but to a lesser degree than if she had complied at step 1. If she doesn't comply, move to step 3. **Do-** Do not repeat the demand. Go over to her and physically prompt her to clean up the toys. Use minimal language and eye contact. Don't lecture her about listening to you, or tell her you don't like it when she ignores you—that's just giving more attention to her noncompliant behavior. If you need to, move your daughter's hands or arms to pick up the toys. Ignore any behaviors she may exhibit such as crying, hitting, flopping to the ground, etc. Do not provide praise or reinforcement once she is done. I also suggest telling your friends and family that while they may mean well, it's best if they let you handle your daughter's behaviors. Their reactions could be reinforcing your daughter's noncompliance.

#100 Birthday Parties

"I dread taking my son to birthday parties. He is in Pre-K, and it seems he gets invited to a birthday party every other week! He almost always will find an isolated corner far away from all the other children and just stim and jump up and down. He doesn't participate in the party at all, and we usually just end up leaving early."

Birthday parties, which can be so much fun and excitement for typically developing children, can be a sensory nightmare for children with Autism. Just think about it: kid's birthday parties are full of loud noises, strangers, music, singing, running children, screams and laughter, and smells. For a child who is sensory sensitive, this can be extremely overwhelming. I have had many clients who go to a birthday party, immediately find the one room with no children in it, and just stim until its time to leave. It is going to take some work to get your child involved in the party, but it's definitely possible. When you arrive at the party, don't just let your child run off or wander away. Walk him through the whole party and point out areas to him, like the food table, the play area, the present table, etc. Present 2 choices to your child of what he wants to do first (since he's young, its best to limit his choice options). Say to him "Do you want to look at the presents or go swing?" If he doesn't choose something, then you pick for him, "Okay, let's go swing." Take your child to the swings and stay there with him to be sure he actually swings and doesn't just wander off to avoid other children. You can alternate between offering choices to your son, and letting him play independently. When you let him play independently its okay if he retreats to a quiet area and stims; that's his way of calming himself down in a stimulating, loud environment. Just don't allow him to stim the entire party. After a few minutes, go over to him and present him with 2 new activities to choose from. This alternating between participating in the party and engaging in stims will allow your child to be able to stay at the party much longer than if you don't allow him to stim at all.

#101 Going to the Movies

"I have a client who I take out into the community every few days. He loves going to the movies, but he gets excited and wants to stand up and jump. If we're the only ones in the movie theatre I let him, but I don't want him disturbing other people trying to watch the movie."

It's important to be consistent when responding to a behavior. By sometimes letting your client stand up and jump and sometimes telling him to sit down, you're sending a mixed message. If you want him to sit and watch the movie, then has to do that all the time—even if the theatre is empty. Start working on this skill at home, it will make it much easier. Watch a DVD with your client in his home, and require him to stay seated during the movie. If he stands up, don't turn the DVD off until he sits back down. That's a common mistake many therapists make. You can't turn the movie off in a movie theatre, so that won't generalize well. If he stands up, tell him to sit back down or the DVD will be "All done". If he sits back down and stays seated, provide praise and tell him he's doing a good job. If he continues to stand up, turn the DVD off and go do something else. Once you turn the DVD off, he can't go back and watch it again for the remainder of the day. This will generalize to public settings much better, because if he keeps standing up inside the movie theatre you can walk out of the theatre and tell him the movie is "All done".

10 Things Your ABA Therapist Wishes You Knew

I read the book <u>10 Things Your Child with Autism Wishes You Knew</u> as a new therapist many years ago, and it's still a favorite of mine.

Well, I think there are a few things that ABA therapists wish more parents knew that would make the job of providing therapy much easier. The ABA therapists who work with your child may feel too nervous or shy to say these things to you, so I will do the honor of speaking for them (you're welcome!):

10 Things Your ABA Therapist Wishes You Knew:

1. **Communication is the key to a great working relationship.** If you are having problems with your therapist, have issues with their punctuality, or feel they call in sick too much, tell them so. Open and direct communication may feel awkward or harsh, but it's much better to be upfront with the therapist and tell them you aren't happy with their performance than to be silently angry or non-communicative, which creates a hostile work environment.
2. **We don't know everything about everything.** ABA therapists often have a diverse knowledge of Autism information and treatments, but all professionals have limitations to what they know or have experienced. I can say from experience, it can be uncomfortable if a family starts to rely on the ABA therapist as a guru who knows all. It's fine to ask your therapists questions or for their advice about something, but just understand that there is a limit to how much they can help you navigate through the maze of Autism.

3. **The more on board with treatment you are, the easier our job is.** The success of any behavioral intervention is dependent upon the people who will be implementing it. In most situations, the main people implementing any behavior plan are the parents. Parents, we need you to be on board and committed to the treatment plan. If you don't agree with the plan, tell us. If you feel the plan isn't working, tell us. But please don't actively work against us by deciding to handle the behavior "your way" and let the therapist handle it his/her way. To put it another way, *"If you wish to modify your child's behavior, you have to change yours first".*
4. **We are individuals, and we will differ.** Maybe you had that one great therapist who was just like Mary Poppins and had your child singing and skipping and dancing, and ever since she quit you have been trying to find her duplicate. Please let that fantasy go. Each ABA therapist will have strengths and weaknesses, things you like and things you don't like. Its unfair to the new therapists you hire to constantly compare them to previous therapists, or ask them to be more like so-and-so. What is appropriate is to share specific strategies and techniques that the old therapist did and ask the new therapist to incorporate those into sessions. However, some therapists just don't have the personality and temperament to be more firm, or to be more easygoing, or to be more creative. We are all different.
5. **Help us to feel comfortable working in your home.** It is a unique and interesting reality of what ABA therapists do that we are right smack in the middle of families' lives. We work in peoples homes, with their most precious gifts: their children. We see things many people don't see, and hear things that

even close family members or friends don't know about you. Some therapists are uncomfortable getting too close to a family, and other therapists need to have a rapport and bond with a family to feel comfortable. This will differ between therapists. The best way to know if your therapist wishes you didn't confide marital problems to her, or wishes you would be friendlier to him, is to ask. It can't hurt to ask the therapist if there's anything you can do to make them feel more comfortable working in your home.

6. **When the therapist is in the home, defer to them.** Okay, now stay with me. I know this might sound strange to ask a parent to take a backseat to the therapist. There's a good reason for this though. In addition to teaching your child it is important that the therapist establishes instructional control. Instructional control basically means that the child learns that the therapist is in charge of the session, and has access to reinforcement. If you are always interrupting sessions, allow your child to come crying to you, or give your child reinforcing items while the therapist is in the home, you could be undermining the therapists authority. This makes the therapist's job much harder. Deferring to the therapist just means communicating with them (see how important communication is?) to make sure you aren't stepping on their toes.

7. **There is a difference between salary negotiations and haggling.** I would say that for most ABA professionals, the rate we give to you is not written in stone. Sometimes we can modify things or come up with alternatives for families who are really struggling to pay our salary. If we can set up a modified payment arrangement for you then we don't mind doing so. What we do mind is families

who try to haggle, or nickel-and-dime with our salary. Haggling would be inviting the therapist to your child's birthday party, and then asking her to run through a quick session "since she's there anyway". Haggling would be asking the therapist to asses your child and his cousin at the same time, since she already has her assessment kit out. Haggling would be scheduling a parent training session with your therapist, and then inviting several friends who have questions about their own children with Autism. Haggling is any time you are trying to get more service out of the therapist than you are actually paying for, and it's insulting. If you are having financial difficulties, just honestly and openly communicate that to the therapist. You might be surprised at how flexible they are willing to be.

8. **We are not magicians, and we don't carry magic wands.** Placing extra pressure on your ABA therapists to bring about specific changes within a specific time frame will lead to unhappy, stressed out therapists over time. I say "extra" pressure because we already place pressure on ourselves. We want to see the children we work with succeed. It only raises our stress level to work with families who constantly demand to know when certain skills will be taught, or when certain behaviors will stop. ABA therapists don't have magical powers, so we can't tell you when X behavior will stop or when Y behavior will start. What we can tell you is how much progress the child has made towards their goals, and the specific techniques we are using to help them learn. To expect anything more than that is like asking us to wave a magic wand.

9. **We Like Reinforcement Too!** We enjoy praise, compliments, and feedback just like our clients do. I like to tell families, "Compliments are free, give 'em

away!" Am I saying you need to have fresh coffee and warm doughnuts prepared for the therapist every time they arrive at your house? Well I'm not saying **DON'T** do that if you really, really want to, but the point is positive reinforcement is nice to receive. If you make a habit out of taking time to show your therapist that they are appreciated, that you know they have a difficult job, and that you approve of them, it will lead to a happy therapist who enjoys working with you and is pleasant to be around.

10. **Your Child is Annoying Sometimes**. If you just laughed at that statement, you passed the awesome test. If you are offended right now, I regret to inform you that a letter stating you failed the awesome test was just mailed to your home. Parents please don't get offended. Children with Autism are some of the most adorable, smart, creative, curious, interesting, and diverse group of children that anyone could get to teach. They are so different from one another, and figuring out how they learn best can be a fun challenge. **BUT,** they can be annoying too. So to the parents, please forgive us if sometimes we don't stick around after a session to chat with you about our weekend or look at adorable baby photos. Sometimes we therapists just want to see your house getting smaller and smaller in our rearview mirror. It's okay though, because we will go home and dig through our *personal stash of reinforcers* (see the next section), and be back bright and early the next day ready to start over!

My Personal Reinforcer List

I don't just use reinforcement strategies on my clients; I use them on myself too. I apply behavioral principles to everything that I do, and I encourage you to do the same.

There are many things I find reinforcing about my career, that keep me in this field. My clients don't usually say "Thanks Ms. Tameika" or place coins in my tip jar, but when I see them use skills that they didn't have before or make changes for the better, that's a huge motivator for me. Bringing about positive and lasting changes in the life of a child is the best part about what I do.

However, just like my clients there are some days when I need more reinforcement than usual. When I have had a difficult day, a stressful day, a tiring day, or one of those days where 2 different kids bite me in the same spot (yes that actually happened) then I have no other option than to reach into my stash of personal reinforcers so the clouds can part and the sun can shine again! I encourage other professionals to do this as well, and to parents, I think you **absolutely** need a personal stash of reinforcers. Caring for and teaching a child with Autism can be hard, strenuous work. It's okay to give yourself a reward or a motivator to stay focused and happy. Happy teacher= happy student, happy therapist=happy client, and happy parent= happy child.

Video Games/Computer Games- Fun and a great way to de-stress. My favorites are The Sims and Rollercoaster Tycoon.
Spa Pedicure- The massage chair, the jasmine scented foot bath, and some lovely pampering—what's not to like?
Shopping- I never do math calculations in my head as quickly as I do when I'm staring at a "15% off" sign.
Baking- I love to cook, but I especially love to bake. Baking itself is a soothing activity, and the actual cake or pie at the end isn't bad either.
Disney Cartoons- I just love them. My favorites are probably The Little Mermaid and Aladdin.
Sensory Toys- I like to say that all those sensory toys sitting in my office were purchased only for my clients, but I've been known to play with a few light up balls or use a weighted blanket myself...talk about relaxing!
Scented Candles- Grapefruit, Vanilla, Sandalwood, or Lavender...did I mention I like sensory things?
Church- There's nothing like praise and worship to take your mind to a much higher place than your problems or bad days.
80's Pop Music- Love it! Bad days just can't compete against some infectious pop tunes.

Appendix

* FBA Explained

A Functional Behavior Analysis is how an ABA professional (typically a BCBA) determines the cause of any behavior. For laypersons, you can easily conduct a *Functional Behavior Assessment* on your own to find out why a repeat behavior is occurring. The steps to conducting a Functional Behavior Assessment are:

1. **Identify the target behavior**
2. **Gather information and data**
3. **Create a hypothesis to explain the behavior**
4. **Create an intervention based on the hypothesis**
5. **Gather information and data**

Select the behavior you want to intervene on. Use the ABC data sheet to collect data on the behavior to determine what is occurring before and after the behavior. Create an explanation for the function of the behavior based on the results of the data, and design an intervention that will serve the same function for the child but in a more appropriate way. Continue to observe and collect data to make sure your intervention is actually working.

All behavior can be categorized into 4 main possible functions: *To gain attention (attention seeking), to access an activity or tangible item (positive reinforcement), to escape/avoid a task or item (negative reinforcement), or for modulation of sensory needs (automatic reinforcement).*

Sample Interventions for Each Function:

Function of <u>Positive Reinforcement</u>: Provide ways for the child to receive reinforcement other than the inappropriate behavior.

Function of <u>Attention</u>: provide an overabundance of attention when the child is behaving appropriately.

Function of <u>Negative Reinforcement</u>: Teach the child to request a break from working.

Function of <u>Automatic Reinforcement</u>: Incorporate a sensory diet

You will know the intervention you created was successful when the target behavior changes (increase or decrease) in the direction you intended it to change. The popularity of the intervention, the ease of use, and the low cost of the intervention are not reasons to decide if an intervention was successful or not.

* **Autism Explained**

Autism is a disorder that usually appears before 3 years of age, and impacts a child's ability to communicate with others, interact and engage with others, and restricts interests to a few repetitive, stereotypical activities. Autism impacts individuals differently, and there will be much variability from child to child. These children are not all the same, and you can't expect one treatment or technique to work with <u>all</u> children with Autism. Some children with Autism do not speak, but some do. Some children with Autism also have cognitive impairments, and some children with Autism are gifted. Autism can affect the body and brain in many different ways including coordination difficulties, speech impairments, short attention span, gastro-intestinal complications, and more. Behavioral problems are very common in children with Autism due to communication deficits, and difficulties with interacting with and relating to others.

It's important to know the warning signs of Autism, as the prevalence rate in the US is rapidly growing. According to the CDC the most updated prevalence rates of Autism are 1 in 88 children. For boys the rate is 1 in 54 (Autism is more common among males). If you are concerned that a child you love may be exhibiting warning signs for Autism, seek the evaluation of a qualified medical professional immediately.

Autism Warning Signs:

- No big smiles or joyful expressions by six months or thereafter
- No back-and-forth sharing of sounds or other facial expressions by nine months or thereafter
- No babbling by 12 months

- No back-and-forth gestures, such as pointing, reaching, or waving by 12 months
- No words by 16 months
- No two-word meaningful phrases by 24 months
- Any loss of speech or babbling or social skills at any age

* ABA Explained

Applied behavior analysis (ABA) is based on the belief that behavior rewarded is more likely to be repeated, and behavior that is not rewarded is less likely to be repeated. ABA is empirical in that it is data based, and it provides direct measures of performance to determine progress. It's systematic in that the environment is manipulated. At its simplest, ABA is a tool to help children learn how to learn.

ABA is a behavioral treatment, so it is used to intervene on what is measurable and observable, such as attending, talking, aggression, sharing, matching, counting, imitating, and much, much more.

ABA Therapists work with individuals who have Autism or other disabilities. We can work with individuals of all ages, with any severity level. We go wherever we are needed: into the home, into the school, into the daycare, etc. We help educate families on how to deal with behavior, and we advocate for our clients as needed. ABA Therapy is one of the most popular treatment methods for Autism, and is **the** most research supported treatment.

ABA focuses on behavior, and behavior is simply anything that can be measured or observed. ABA can be used to teach, increase or decrease talking, playing with peers, raising a hand in the classroom, shoe tying, attending, and on and on.

What is most important when deciding on a treatment method is to look at the child's needs: What skills do they need in order to have a better quality of life? Select a therapeutic method that will meet those needs. It is important to select a therapeutic method that has empirical data to support it, and has been proven to work with specifically with Autism. It's nice if a therapy works great for children with speech disorder or ADD, but how do you know it will work for a child who has Autism?

There are so many reasons why ABA is the **Gold Standard** of Autism treatment. ABA is a decades old, empirically supported treatment method for children with Autism. The amount of research conducted on ABA is massive. ABA stands out as a treatment method because it specifically addresses behavior, is intended to be implemented in whatever environment the behavior naturally occurs (usually the home), and focuses on skill development.

* Sensory Activity Ideas

Disclaimer: *"These interventions are not behavior-analytic in nature and are not covered by my BACB credential."*

Many children with Autism have sensory modulation issues, which can present as behavioral problems, hyperactiveness, or inattentiveness if you don't know what to look for. Conducting a complete FBA will reveal if a behavior problem is actually a sensory issue, but observing the child closely and looking for patterns will also help you determine between sensory issues and problem behaviors.

Children who are sensory seekers tend to need much stimulation from their environment. This is the student who tries to climb up on their desk, or the child who jumps on the couch while they watch TV.
Children who are sensory avoiders receive too much stimulation form their environment.. This is the student who sticks their fingers in their ears during Circle Time, or the child who hides under their bed when relatives unexpectedly drop by. Understanding the sensory needs of your child, student, or client will help you modify the learning environment and know how to optimize the child's focus and attention.

If the child needs to be calmed: Provide firm massage to the shoulders or back, squeeze their hands firmly between your hands, blow bubbles, listen to calming music or sounds, take the child for a walk lasting 10-15 minutes, give the child a sensory tub or bin to manipulate, blow air into balloons, place a weighted vest in the child's lap, sniff a calming scent such as vanilla, have the child jump on a trampoline, messy play in shaving cream or foamy soap, or do deep breathing exercises.

If the child needs to be "revved" up: Fast or start/stop swinging, tickle fight, Spin the child repeatedly on a chair or toy, listen to upbeat, fast music, let the child hand upside-down from a bar or playground equipment, wrap the child in a blanket like a burrito and roll the child across the floor, race the child up the street and back, walk outside on grass, sand, or pebbles barefoot, sniff alerting scents such as citrus, or have a dance party.

* Hiring ABA Therapists: Interview Tips

Sometimes families are uncomfortable being placed in the position of "Manager" of an in-home ABA program. As the parent, that is what you are. Even if you have a Lead Therapist supervising the program, the parents are the one who make hiring and firing decisions. It's important that you treat the hiring process seriously. The way you interact and communicate with the therapists will send a clear message about the level of professionalism you expect. If you want competent, professional, and dedicated therapists then take the time to recruit carefully and interview thoroughly before hiring anyone. It saves time, effort, and money to be honest with staff upfront about the requirements of the job, and your expectations of an ABA therapist.

If you hire a company to provide therapy services to your child, or if your child receives ABA at school then typically you won't be interviewing staff. The school or agency will decide who will be working with your child. If you run your own in-home ABA program, then you are responsible for selecting, training, and supervising staff. Many parents are unsure of what to ask during the interview process as well as what characteristics and traits to look for when hiring ABA professionals. Here are some tips for you:

Decide before you meet with any potential therapist the job expectations, schedule, minimum and maximum pay rate, and create a short summary of daily job responsibilities. Ask plenty of questions beyond what the resume tells you. Schedule the interview for a time when your child will be home, and observe interaction between the potential therapist and your child. Consider including an employment clause where the individual agrees to a minimum length of employment, such as one year.
- o Suggested interview topics to discuss: Motivation for doing this kind of work, Autism knowledge, ABA experience, philosophy of education, future career goals, minimum pay desired, availability, health/physical

limitations, program goals, strengths and weaknesses, experience with this kind of work (if no experience, willing to attend non-paid trainings?).

- o   Signs of a great ABA professional:
- He/she is passionate about their work, enjoys talking about ABA strategies and principles with you, and sharing techniques with you.
- He/she seems to genuinely like, *not just tolerate*, being around children. You see or hear the therapist laughing and having fun with your child before or after sessions. They don't just finish the session, clean up, and head home.
- He/she talks about career goals within ABA or a related field. It isn't just a "job" to them; it is a career path they are interested in.
- He/she becomes emotionally invested in your child's progress. If you have been struggling for months with toilet training, and you call the therapist excited one night that your child just peed in the potty the therapist will be excited with you.
- He/she asks for feedback and supervision. If no supervisor is available they seek out books, movies, or research articles about ABA, Autism, behavior, etc, so they can increase their knowledge.
- He/she is a team player, and open to communication with the child's teacher or related therapists (Speech Therapist, Occupational Therapist, etc.).
- He/she responds appropriately to suggestions for improvement and constructive criticism. They do not respond by being defensive or becoming upset. They want to learn how to perform their job well.
- He/she has an open mind regarding approaches, strategies, interventions, or methods of behavior management. If you tell the therapist you are considering a supplemental therapy, they are interested in the treatment and even if not in support of it, they have an open mind regarding it.

- He/she is a consistent individual. They show up on time, work the full session (doesn't consistently leave early), call when they say they will call, attend required staff meetings, etc. It is apparent that they take their job seriously and are a professional.

* ABC Data Behavior Form

The A-B-C's of behavior is a basic tool used in ABA to determine the function, or motivation (from the child's perspective) of a behavior. A behavior intervention that is created based on the function of a behavior will be more successful than if the function is not known.

A= Antecedent. This means what occurred before the behavior

B=Behavior. This is the actual behavior

C=Consequence. This means what happened after the behavior

Date & Time	Therapist Initials	Antecedent *What happened before the behavior?*	Behavior *Describe the behavior*	Consequence *What happened after the behavior?*

References

Baker, J. E. (2008). No More Meltdowns. Arlington, TX: Future Horizons, Inc.

Cooper, J.O., Heron, T.E., & Heward, W.L. (2007). Applied Behavior Analysis (2nd Edition). Upper Saddle River, NJ: Pearson.

Kranowitz, C. (1998). The Out-of-Sync Child: Recognizing and Coping with Sensory Integration Dysfunction. New York: Perigee Book.

Lovaas, O.I. (1987) "Behavioral treatment and normal educational and intellectual functioning in young autistic children." Journal *of Consulting and Clinical Psychology, 55*, 3-9

Notbohm, E. (2005). Ten Things Every Child with Autism Wishes You Knew. TX: Future Horizons, Inc.

www.Iloveaba.com

www.autismspeaks.org

http://www.cdc.gov/

http://www.thegraycenter.org/social-stories

Made in the USA
Middletown, DE
15 January 2019